Get Streaming with Amazon Video Direct

A guide to AVD for independent creators from someone who has actually done it.

Ralph W. Bagnall

Discover more about Ralph Bagnall at Woodcademy.com and ConsultingWoodworker.com.

Contents

Introduction

The first episode of my Amazon Video Direct show, Woodcademy (Woodcademy.com/WCTV), began streaming on June 1, 2017. It was remarkably exciting for me and the culmination of many months of work and preparation. Amazon had spun AVD off of their CreateSpace self publishing platform in November 2016, so there were no guides or books available on how to manage the system beyond Amazon's own support documents.

I wrote this book to help fill in some of the blanks left in these Amazon Video Direct (AVD) support documents. I also talk about some of the issues I encountered along the way that are not explained as well as a new user might need. These include challenges like the video formats and subtitle files that seem like they should work but don't, and issues around Amazon's rules against "advertising", which I will discuss in detail. Although AVD provides an email address that can be used to submit questions, my experience has been that the replies are generally just a copy and paste of relevant sections from the support documents; contacting AVD through this method usually shed little to no light on my questions.

I strongly advise you to take the time to read through all of the support documentation on the AVD site (videodirect.amazon.com). This will be VERY helpful, not only for setting up your account and learning how to navigate the site, but also for understanding and following along with this guide. I'm not going to go into great detail on the information included in the AVD support documentation as it is readily accessible to anyone who wishes to read it. However, I do include excerpts from the support documents in this guide where relevant.

This book is not a guide to the process of shooting and producing your show or movie for Amazon Video Direct. There are many great guides out there and while I do create content professionally, I am a furniture maker first, and a videographer a long way second. If you happen to be a novice producer, I highly recommend *How to Shoot Video that Doesn't Suck* (amzn.to/2vOV3Cg) by Steven Stockman. It is an excellent guide to the strategies of shooting good video as opposed to a technical manual on videography. After more than a decade of shooting video for manufacturers and retailers in the woodworking space and for my YouTube channel (bit.ly/2DFQIAW), I can tell you that HOW you shoot is much more important that WHAT equipment you use to make the shot. (If you would like more info on the details of my video work, please feel free to contact me via the Woodcademy website and I will be happy to discuss it.)

Neither is this book meant to be a definitive work covering every possible aspect of using Amazon Video Direct. The service is very new, and I have only a single season of my own show uploaded as of this writing. I learned enough through this process that by the time I completed the third episode, I was able to successfully upload everything for the show in one try. But while my experience is limited, so is everyone else's. I could find only one book on using Amazon Video Direct when I searched in early 2017 and it was literally just a copy of Amazon's own support documentation with pronoun changes from "our" to "their". It was not at all helpful during my learning curve.

This book is designed to share my experiences with the AVD system, and hopefully help you avoid some of the hurdles I had to overcome. I spent many hours over the course of several months figuring out how to structure the actual video formatting to be accepted, creating a proper closed caption file, and why my files were being rejected during Amazon's content review process. I don't claim to be an expert on all topics surrounding getting your program onto AVD. Think of me as more of a guide, a "Sherpa" who has climbed the mountain at least once, and can share with you the pitfalls I have already encountered and how I worked around them.

Again, I need to stress that the information in this book will be easier to understand, and your experience with AVD smoother, if you take the time to first read through the Amazon Video Direct Support Documents located at videodirect.amazon.com.

Marketplace

I published my first YouTube video in 2006, so I was on the cutting edge of that revolution. And while my YouTube woodworking channel provides a lot of benefit to my business, I had never directly monetized it, and really did not capitalize on this early adopter phase as I could or should have. Back then, there weren't very many content providers on YouTube and the audience for YouTube was just a fraction of what it is now. In 2006 a much smaller segment of the population had heard of YouTube, and it was only viewable on a computer hard wired to the Internet. In the Amazon Video Direct space, I am quite literally in on the ground floor again - and you can be too.

The big difference now is that Amazon's Prime Video service has a huge audience of viewers already watching, and they are looking for great content on all types of devices. This rare situation cannot help but to offer unique opportunities to producers, especially those of us in the early stages of creating content for this platform.

There are very clear parallels between the history of the print publishing marketplace and the video marketplace. For most of human history, access to printing has been very limited. You had to have your own press, submit letters to newspapers, or convince one of a very few publishing houses that your content was marketable and worth risking loads of money to publish.

Desktop publishing, WordPress, and other Internet publishing formats turned the print publishing world on its head, and now anyone can easily and inexpensively be published widely. Even after the Internet revolution of digital publishing, getting a book physically printed without selling it to an editor was known as "vanity press" and required substantial funds to get a minimum number of copies printed in the hope that you could sell enough to get your investment back.

In the publishing world, Amazon's CreateSpace Service (createspace.com) became an answer for numerous authors. CreateSpace is "Print on Demand". There is virtually no upfront money needed to get your book published, and because they are only printed to order, no author need be stuck with hundreds of paid for but unsold books. Physical books are printed only when an order is placed. Amazon gets paid BEFORE printing so the author need not come up with any money at all. Amazon also supplies a customized individual shopping cart page, and handles all the transactions, sales taxes, etc. It's a perfect vehicle for the beginning author or those whose subject matter is too narrowly defined to attract publishers. Print on demand is also more environmentally friendly than printing copies because there is little to no waste. No book is printed until an order is received.

Your CreateSpace books can be sold by you in person, or on your own site. Better yet, they are listed and sold on Amazon.com. I currently have three titles published through CreateSpace, and though my books are available directly on my website (Woodcademy.com/book-store-1), most months I sell more through Amazon.com than on my own website. If you are not already familiar with CreateSpace, you should be, because there are many ways your video efforts might be augmented through print and eBooks. Again, I won't go into the how-to here, as there are many good resources (amzn.to/2vOo8xK) available already.

The evolution of video has followed a similar path, with television networks, movie studios and ad agencies as the gatekeepers that had to be convinced to spend the enormous funds needed to create even a few minutes of on-air content. Then digital cameras appeared, editing could be done with software, and YouTube, Vimeo and similar services became platforms where anyone can get their work screened, and the world of moving pictures was as disrupted as publishing had been previously.

In both the blogosphere and the YouTube/Vimeo universe, the sheer volume of content generated by free access for everyone lends each venue a perception of lesser value and quality. And with tens of millions of blog posts and videos online, it can be VERY difficult to rise above the noise, even with excellent quality work.

Affordable Video Distribution for All

In 2016, Amazon Video Direct was spun off from CreateSpace, allowing video producers the opportunity to have their productions available for streaming from Amazon's Prime Video service at no cost to the producer. In fact, Amazon actually pays the producer (you) based on viewing numbers even if the videos are offered free.

YouTube is wonderful and has been VERY good for my business, but there is a perceived quality difference in the public mind between a video on YouTube and a program streamed on Amazon Prime. This perception may or may not stand the test of time, but for now it exists, it is very real, and it should allow early adopters the ability to capitalize on it for the foreseeable future. More on this idea later.

What, Exactly, Is AVD?

Interestingly, even the AVD main page has no specific description of what Amazon Video Direct really is, so here's my best shot at it. As I see it, Amazon Video Direct is a self–publishing platform for television programs and movies. You can literally shoot your own movie or TV episode and, without having to pay anyone, make it available for people to stream on Amazon Prime. Believe me, I FULLY realize that the time and money investment in producing your own show is not small, but Amazon doesn't charge for carrying it on their Prime Video platform. In fact, they pay you to stream it.

From Amazon Support, Account Setup FAQs:

"What can I publish?": You can publish professionally produced videos that you own and are interested in monetizing. We accept all video types including short/long

form movies, TV series, web series, digital shorts, music videos, news, sports, educational videos, fitness programs, and more. The subject matter can span a diverse range of genres and categories.

As far as I can tell from the Amazon support documents, there are no minimum or maximum time restrictions on shows there. This may have some interesting implications in the future, and if shorter or longer time frames work for your content, you should explore them. But for now it seems that "shows" are sticking to a 20-60 minute format, and "movies" run an hour or longer. My show, Woodcademy, is a half-hour format program, with an actual run time of 25-30 minutes. My show is an experiment to see if I can garner a reasonably sized audience for an independent woodworking TV show. Should I prove that I can, I want to be in the best position to edit the existing content to fit the traditional TV model so my shows could air on HGTV or similar how-to oriented networks. In other words, I want to be at least close enough in time to insert advertising without having to cut out too much of the content. I don't know that this will happen, or that I will want to go this route even if it is offered, but as you delve into this very new opportunity, keep in mind that the rules are still being written, so stay as flexible as you possibly can and watch for opportunities as they present themselves.

AVD Vs. YouTube

Right now I can hear some of you saying, "So what? I've been doing all that on YouTube for years, why bother with all the extra rules imposed by Amazon to get onto Prime?" I believe the answer lies in what I see as the four main advantages AVD has over YouTube: *Competition, Perception, Quality and Length.*

Competition

While getting your video production on AVD doesn't cost you beyond production costs, there are some pretty impressive technical and content hurdles you need to get over before Amazon will accept and approve your production for streaming. Whereas anyone can post pretty much anything they like on YouTube, (excluding nudity or racist content) there is no review process for videos being uploaded. Videos can be uploaded that violate YouTube's rules or even Federal law, and remain viewable until it is brought to the attention of YouTube and they determine to take it down. YouTube allows linking and advertising, and they actively encourage it, making monetizing your content quite easy.

Additionally, no one at YouTube is monitoring or cares about whether titles match content or even if the thumbnail is at all relevant to the video. We have all seen videos with explosions, wrecks or scantily clad women in the thumbnails only to find out the video has nothing to do with the image used.

In contrast, every video uploaded to AVD is held for review by Amazon and simply will not be made public until it meets Amazon's guidelines. The closed caption file requirement alone is enough to keep most casual producers off the site. (See the Closed Captions section for more on this.) As I will also explain later, Amazon is VERY strict about what they call *advertising*, and that makes it much more difficult to directly monetize your video content. Therefore, most content creators who might compete with you for audience attention on YouTube or Vimeo are unlikely to make the transition to AVD.

Perception

To be honest, my Woodcademy show on Amazon Prime features the same host, (yours truly) shooting the same topics with the same equipment as in my videos posted on YouTube. From a practical standpoint, there is no ACTUAL difference in the quality of the content or the production values. But I believe that there is a very strong PERCEIVED difference in the collective mind of the general public that YouTube is an amateur platform, whereas Amazon Prime is for professionals.

I can tell a stranger all about my YouTube channel (bit.ly/2DFQIAW) with its 150+ woodworking videos, 7500 subscribers and 2.4 million views, and they might show a little interest if they happen to be or know a woodworker; but only a little. When I tell that same stranger about my Woodworking TV show on Amazon Prime, the reaction is quite different. The interest level is much higher. The fact that my independently produced woodworking show is streaming on Amazon Prime surprises and amazes them. The difference matters. The PLATFORM matters. The "Media is the Message" in this case.

It is the same concept I find as a freelance woodworking author. Anyone can put up a woodworking blog, but being published in a national magazine carries a much higher perceived value with the audience. The public sees the magazine as a curator, helping to insure the content is of a given level of quality and accuracy that self publishing simply does not have.

A good deal of the perception is also directly traceable back to the fact that until now, virtually all content available through Prime has been professional material produced by professional studios. Amazon's viewing list consists primarily of recognized movies and TV shows the viewing public already knows or has heard about.

At this point, publishing your show on AVD is sort of like sneaking your demo tape into the playlist of a nationally broadcast radio station. It would have to have distinctly bad production values to be spotted as an impostor by the audience, so anyone hearing it will automatically assume that it is a professionally produced track.

Quality

Continuing my radio station analogy, it's highly unlikely that the production values of anything AVD approves will be poor enough to immediately reveal the "snuck in demo". The content may or may not be compelling, (THAT is up to you) but production values WILL be held to a standard. While AVD is currently not streaming 4K video, they are certainly favoring high definition video with good frame rates. They currently accept 640x480 with a 4:3 aspect ratio, but I suspect not for too much longer. Their software automatically adjusts the delivery stream to match the device, but a growing number of viewers are watching Prime on high def TVs, and SD video is simply not going to look good on the big screen. For that matter, it looks bad on any decent tablet these days. Additionally, the work involved in creating the Closed Caption file yourself, or the cost of having it done, is too much to waste on second rate quality.

So at least for the time being, the quality of programs streaming on Prime are held to a higher standard than YouTube, and I believe Amazon is seriously committed to keeping things this way to protect their Prime brand.

Length

Online viewing times on YouTube, Vimeo and similar services are certainly climbing. When I began in 2006, 90 seconds was the line where viewers began clicking through to the next video, even with compelling content. But as of today, viewers will stick around for 7-10 minutes at a time if the content is good. While there are certainly longer format videos being watched through these sites, they are not the norm. Most people still prefer to watch longer programs on larger screens. And while there are many ways to watch what is on a mobile device on your big screen TV, Amazon Prime is easily watched through their Fire device, game consoles or directly through a smart TV, and these methods leave mobile devices free to be used while watching Prime shows as is quickly becoming the norm. In the case of Woodcademy TV it works to our advantage, as a viewer can have the episode's companion PDF project plan (Woodcademy.com/WCTV) open on their tablet and use it to follow along while watching the program. Again, all of this is subject to change, but for now, these are the realities.

I had an early viewer tell me that he watched the first four minutes of my first episode on his laptop, but liked it so much that he stopped so he could watch it later at home on his big screen TV, something he does not do with YouTube videos. I can easily watch YouTube directly on my TV through my game console but rarely do. 98% of my YouTube viewing is on my iPad or laptop, and often while I am watching something else on the television.

With Woodcademy, I have already seen a trend toward short viewing habits over the 8 months of data available. On any given day, the minutes streamed divided by the number of unique streaming sessions indicates that people tend to watch my show in 12-15 minute blocks even though each episode is about a half hour long. As I explain later, the statistics cannot prove this, but the ratio of 12-15 minutes per unique stream has remained the same even as the minutes streamed has steadily grown from a few minutes a day to over 1000 minutes.

If your show is specifically geared toward younger audiences, you may find that young adults are far more comfortable watching on tablets or phones, even when a larger television screen is available. This doesn't mean they don't watch shows and movies on Amazon Prime. They certainly do, but you might want to take smaller screens into account when creating and editing your content.

AVD Dashboard and Reporting

The AVD Dashboard you use to upload your files and track their viewership is disappointingly sparse. This is especially true when compared to Amazon's retail operation metrics which are top notch. I have an Amazon affiliate account and books published and sold through CreateSpace and Kindle, and I have become used to a high standard. I believe that the current lack of dashboard quality is because AVD is pretty new and I remain hopeful that the dashboard will improve over time.

Currently, metrics available include viewing by minutes streamed and the unique number of streams. These measures are available only by day, and are reported in periods of the last 7 days, 4 weeks or 12 weeks. A filter for a custom period is not yet available. In point of fact, the "7 Days" option so far has virtually never shown 7 days of data. Typically, this time selection shows 5-6 days of results, sometimes only 4. I suspect this is due to the vagaries of reporting content viewed offline. (See below) You can also filter the results viewed by all offers (*Prime, Free with Ads, Purchases, Rentals and Subscriptions*).

This limited and constantly moving range of metrics make it more difficult to record and compare streaming numbers over any time period of more than three consecutive months when using the dashboard. The only way to check quarter-over–quarter in the dashboard is to screen capture or otherwise record the dashboard at twelve week intervals and manually compare them. Otherwise you'll need to download and compile the info month-to-month.

To do the latter, the Dashboard *does* allow you to export the metrics as a .csv file by month, so you can record and compare totals, but it would be nice to simply do everything within the website like you can with email software or web hosting. If you know how, or know someone who does, you can import these .csv files into a spreadsheet. The one my wife designed tracks each month and produces a chart clearly showing the view rates at a glance. This is VERY helpful for talking to advertisers or sponsors as we will discuss later.

Another thing to note is that the metrics are not updated in real time. The viewing numbers seem to typically be updated once or twice each day, but checking stats each morning can be challenging as the numbers reported can change. When a viewer downloads your program to offline later, the download is not what is recorded. The record of actual viewing time is held in the device until it is next connected to the Internet, and then reported. In other words, a viewer who downloads the show to watch on a plane later is not counted even as this viewer takes the flight and watches the show. The minutes viewed are not recorded by Amazon until this viewer's device connects to the Internet once again and automatically reports the viewing data to Amazon. This explains at least some of the delay in reporting and changes to the daily numbers.

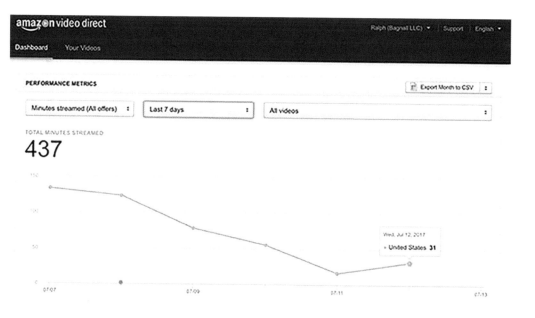

Typically, the daily streaming numbers reported can change up to a week after the date has passed. For example, on Thursday, July 13 (above), the streaming count for Wednesday, July 12, showed 31 minutes of streaming, but the final count for the 12th ended up being 196 minutes streamed as reported on July 20 (below).

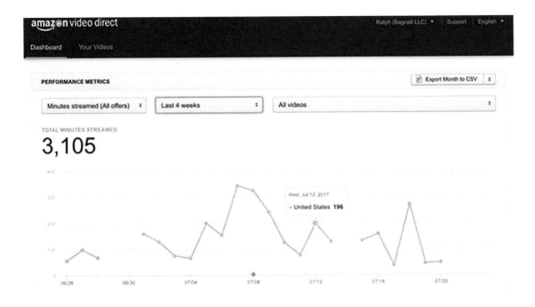

The metrics on the Dashboard count minutes streamed and unique viewers. You can break out these numbers by Prime, Free with Ads and Subscriptions, but that is pretty much it. I can only see the metrics for the full season I have available on Prime; no provisions on the dashboard exist for viewing the metrics for individual episodes. There is no way to determine which demographics are watching, how long any individual watches at any one time, what times of day viewing takes place, or the devices used for viewing.

From Amazon Support, Glossary:

Unique streams is the total count of unique streaming sessions. It's the same as the total count of customer Play button clicks. For example, if a customer starts watching a title in a web browser, switches to a mobile device, and then continues on Fire TV it's counted as three unique streams.

The Unique Streams metric is NOT the overall number of individuals who watch your show, or even the number of devices used to watch. It is actually a record of every incidence of someone watching any part of your show(s) on Amazon. For example, in the week of July 17-23, my dashboard reports 31 Unique Streams and 396 minutes streamed. This could be 31 people watching 13 minutes each, 14 people watching all 28 minutes of an episode in two sessions each, or even one person watching the show over and over 12 minutes at a time. There is currently no way of knowing, and with multiple episodes, it is impossible to determine on the dashboard.

Earnings

The Dashboard presents info on your earnings, but it is listed as an estimate even after the period is completed. The only firm earnings number is what has already been paid.

Electronic Transfer directly to your bank account is Amazon's preferred method of payment, and unless there is a very compelling reason not to, you should use this method. If you choose wire transfer, it is important to note that AVD is currently only making deposits when the payment meets a

$100.00 USD threshold for US accounts (threshold varies based on country/currency).

From Amazon Support, Payments and Banking:

All Amazon Video Direct payments are made through Electronic Funds Transfer (EFT) or wire transfer.

When converting local royalty earnings to a different currency for an EFT payment, the amount to be paid after conversion must meet the minimum amount your indicated bank will allow us to send. This amount varies by institution and location. However, once the minimum amount is reached, you will be paid electronically for the full amount accrued.

Local Marketplace	Threshold
Amazon.com	$100
Amazon.co.uk	£100
Amazon.de	€100
Amazon.co.jp	¥10,000

Wire transfer payments will be dispersed after they reach the minimum applicable threshold by marketplace.

You will not receive a wire transfer payment for any amounts below these thresholds.

When converting local royalty earnings to a different currency or withholding any applicable tax, the amount to be paid after conversion/withholding must meet the above requirements.

For more information, please see Royalty Information.
(videodirect.amazon.com)

Exporting Data

The metrics reported can be exported as a .csv file, and as mentioned earlier, this is currently the best way you can track your show's metrics over time. We convert each file to an Excel workbook with tabs identifying the individual spreadsheets by month. These spreadsheets are more detailed than the dashboard and cover the entire month, so they are much more useful. Episodes of a series are listed separately, so that is very helpful because you can sort or filter by episode, but again, there is no practical way to determine the true number of individual viewers who are watching. While the data exported in this .csv file from Amazon doesn't provide totals, it isn't difficult to modify each spreadsheet to provide that information.

Get Started Using AVD

The first step is to set up an account. You can use your existing Prime account or create a new one. Again, I don't need to cover all this in detail since AVD has step by step instructions already available.

You will need to choose how to monetize your program, and there are several options. They are clearly explained in the Support Documents, and I cover monetization in depth later. If you plan to make your content *Free with Prime Membership*, you will also have the option for making it *Free with Pre-Roll Ads*. This means that people WITHOUT a Prime membership can also watch your program at no charge; they just see Amazon-inserted advertising with the program. As widespread as Amazon Prime is, it is not yet universal. I chose this option so that anyone with an Internet connection can watch my show. I want as many viewers as possible, and you receive 55% of whatever revenues Amazon makes from the ads they insert with your video when a non-member views it.

Uploading Files

The Dashboard is also where you upload files and track where you are in the process. You first need to decide the category your content fits within. There are three publishing categories in the AVD system: Stand Alone, Episodic and Subscription.

Stand Alone:

This is for a single production that is not part of a larger set of titles such as a TV series. Think movies, film shorts, music videos, and documentaries.

Episodic:

As you might expect, this is the category for "TV Show" type content. Here you upload seasons that contain multiple episodes. You can add a season of episodes as a group or start a season and add episodes as you wish. I am presenting Woodcademy through the as-you-go method at present, creating and adding episodes one at a time. If you have a miniseries or multi-part documentary, you may want to load them as a series with all episodes within one season.

Subscription:

To be honest, I am a bit unclear of exactly what a subscription is or why you might want to set one up. Perhaps this could be a model for paid educational content. It does offer some interesting possibilities if you have a program that can benefit from this publishing method, but since the subscription is not available within Prime in the US, it is something of a mystery to me.

From Amazon Support, Publish a Subscription:

> *You can create one U.S.-based subscription per account. A subscription must contain a minimum of 30 titles and remain available for a minimum of 18 months. Titles included in a subscription aren't eligible to be included with Prime in the United States.*

Availability

When I started streaming my show, there were four regions to choose from where it could be offered; US, Great Britain, Germany and Japan. I saw no reason not to offer it in all regions, and in fact often got more views from Germany than from Great Britain.

As of October 2017, Amazon requires that translations be provided for at least one of the primary languages for each region. That means I would need to provide a Japanese version and/or a German version to stream my show in those areas. I simply do not get enough streaming from either to make it work the cost and effort. So my show now only streams to the US and Great Britain.

From Amazon Support, Caption (timed text) Information:

What are the language requirements for publishing?

Catalog Listing
The Catalog Listing Language for a title must be one of a location's supported languages to publish to that location (English for the United States and United Kingdom, German for Germany, and Japanese for Japan).

The Catalog Listing Language for a title must be the same as either the audio or caption language.

File Formats Needed

There are just a few files required for any of the publishing programs, including your video file, closed caption file and a few images for the various title pages on Amazon. These all need to be uploaded before publishing. Fortunately, if anything gets rejected, you only need to reload the rejected file(s). This is important to understand as your video file is likely to take some time to upload, while the images and closed caption files take seconds. So, unless the issue is with the video file, uploading again is fairly quick and painless.

Mezzanine File

The video file you upload is called a "Mezzanine file". This refers to a convention that ensures your file is standardized enough to work within the Amazon system. If you are interested in learning more, Bruce Devlin of AmberFin does a pretty good job explaining in his Bruce's Shorts series on YouTube (youtu.be/09s_MORhGY4). If you are using high def video, and you absolutely should be, the mezzanine file will take some time to upload.

Your video file can be uploaded as one of several file types. Be sure to render your video into one of the appropriate formats AND the proper "container". I initially used an accepted codec but missed the part that said the .mov wrapper is not accepted. Trial and error turns out to be an arduous process and you want to avoid it, especially with the video upload. My HD video files, at around 28 minutes in length, run to 6 or 7 gigabytes, and even with the business class upload speeds at my office, the files take about an hour to upload. My basic home Internet simply choked on the file and gave up! Remember that we typically buy our internet services based on fast download speeds, but as a video producer, you will need much better upload capacity than a typical consumer internet account provides.

Once uploaded, it can take from several hours to several days to find out if the file is rejected or not on TECHNICAL grounds. As you can imagine, this process can be frustrating, especially as Amazon does not provide specific reasons for rejection, or any advice on how to fix it outside of advising you to re-render the file in a different format.

From Amazon Support, Mezzanine Requirements:

Codecs and file formats

AVC/H.264

- **Supported Containers**: .mp4, .m2t, .ts
  Note   H.264 video in .mov wrappers aren't supported.
- **Profile**: High
- **Recommended Bitrate for HD Resolution**: 30 Mbps
- **Recommended Bitrate for SD Resolution**: 15 Mbps
- **Key Frame Interval**: 2 seconds (or less)
- **Audio Format**: AC-3 or AAC
- **Recommended Bitrate for AC-3 Audio:**
  - 5.1 – Bitrate: 448 Kbps, Sample Rate: 48 kHz
  - Stereo – Bitrate: 192 Kbps, Sample Rate: 48 kHz
- **Recommended Bitrate for AAC Audio:**
  - 5.1 – Bitrate: 768 Kbps, Sample Rate: 48 kHz
  - Stereo – Bitrate: 320 Kbps, Sample Rate: 48 kHz

MPEG-2

- **Supported Containers**: .mpg, .mpeg, .m2p, .m2t, .m2ts, .ts
- **Profile**: Main
- **Recommended Bitrate for HD Resolution**: 80 Mbps
- **Recommended Bitrate for SD Resolution**: 50 Mbps
- **Key Frame Interval**: 1-second or less. I-Frame only preferred.
- **Audio Format**: PCM or MPEG Layer II
- **Recommended Bitrate for PCM Audio**:
  - 5.1 – Lossless, Sample Rate: 48 kHz
  - Stereo - Lossless, Sample Rate: 48 kHz
- **Recommended Bitrate for MPEG Layer II Audio**:
  - 5.1 – Data Rate: 768 Kbps, Sample Rate: 48 kHz
  - Stereo – Bitrate: 384 Kbps, Sample Rate: 48 kHz

Pro-Res 422

- **Supported Containers**: .mov
- **Profile**: HQ
- **Recommended Bitrate for HD Resolution**: 220 Mbps
- **Recommended Bitrate for SD Resolution**: 110 Mbps
- **Key Frame Interval**: Not applicable. Pro-Res files are I-Frame only.
- **Audio Format**: PCM
- **Recommended Audio Bitrate**: Lossless, Sample Rate: 48 kHz

The Amazon Support Documents contain more specific information, and reviewing them carefully will save you a lot of grief.

Closed Captioning

A lthough AVD often uses the term subtitles, they are really after a true closed caption file, not just subtitles scrolling on the screen. You simply are not able to submit your project without a properly formatted closed caption file. As I expressed in the first chapter, I am convinced this will be the first barrier to all the folks posting on YouTube making the leap to AVD. It can be a serious challenge to create a proper CC file.

First off, most free video editing software packages are not capable of creating a proper CC file. I currently use Corel Video Studio 10, a reasonably priced video editing program. Although it allows for creating the CC file, it is a completely manual process accomplished by picking the start and end point of each line of text within the video, then typing the text by hand. My first episode, at 28 minutes long, took more than 10 hours to create the CC file. As I learned how to use the CC feature in my software, I got faster, but episodes still take around 6 hours to create. Now, it may be possible to create the text using speech-to-text software, but I haven't as yet explored the feasibility of doing so in Video Studio 10.

There is software on the market designed to create CC files, but the inexpensive ones start at $150.00 and increase from there, and they use the same manual method as I am using now. The better ones can manage speech-to-text conversions, but prices start above $2000.00 and still need to be edited for personal names and uncommon technical terms such as my woodworking show uses. I haven't tried any of these yet. If my show's streaming data justifies it, then this type of software will be a worthy investment, but certainly not just starting out.

Having It Done

If you have read the Amazon support pages, you know that they recommend having the captions created by a third party service, and provide links to several such services. This is a viable option if you have the budget for it, but as I am pioneering this process, I prefer to "fail fast and cheap", putting in time rather than money until I've proven the concept viable. Once I can prove the value of my show (*more on this in "Monetizing"*) then I'll look into either having the captions created for me or investing in software that can do it automatically.

The end result of your closed captioning efforts is actually a simple text file, but one with specific details. Each line of text to appear on the screen must be preceded by a sequential caption number, the exact start time in the video stream down to three decimal places, the text to appear, and the end time, also carried out to three decimal places.

There are no (as far as I can find) hard and fast rules for how many words or characters should appear on the screen at one time, nor how long each timed Caption section should be. I prefer to have 5-8 words per caption clip depending on length. To get some feel for what you like and do not like, try turning on the Closed Captions on your TV and watch the results.

Especially with dramas, I have seen "lazy" Closed Captioning that misses words, misspells words or even gets the words wrong. Also, if the timing is off, it can be very annoying and even spoil plot points when the words appear before they are actually spoken. With a how-to show like mine, this is not so much an issue, but I try to have the caption match the speech as closely as possible.

I also pay attention to how numbers are presented. Being a how-to show, I speak both measurements and numbers of items. Spelling out the item numbers while using the actual numbers for measurements helps the viewer keep track. As an example, I would say, "cut twelve parts at 12 inches long" rather than "cut 12 parts at 12 inches long". I also often use a wireless lapel mic to talk through the operations as I do them rather than adding a voice over later. This sometimes results in long pauses between words even in a single sentence when I am talking and doing at the same time. When this happens, I like to add a series of three periods to let the viewer know that the thought is not yet complete. For example; "the glue is the applied… and the parts clamped together." These two phrases appear as separate captions, often with several seconds between, but the viewer knows they are connected.

Nothing is so confusing and annoying as poor grammar and punctuation. Poor grammar should be written out as is when captioning character dialog. Otherwise, proper grammar and punctuation should be used for Closed Captioning.

One final note - do not forget to include a description of sounds. Personally, I only do this to avoid confusion when there is no talking going on. In these instances, I just add a simple description of the sound enclosed between parentheses like this: (table saw)

Whether you create your own CC file, or have it done, you will want to proof read it very carefully. Amazon reviews this file just as diligently as they will the video. I submitted a CC file that was missing two phrases totaling about 10 words in a 30 minute video and they caught it even though I had not. We have all seen Closed Captions on large budget shows that have errors, especially with technical terms or proper names, so review the files made for you just as carefully as those you create yourself and save the time involved in resubmitting.

Formats

Amazon specifies a number of different CC file formats it will accept, but I found that my software outputs in a .srt file that, while a correct option, still got rejected. Note that Amazon does not tell you WHY it got rejected, just that it did.

Format Issues

While the Amazon support documents show this format as one distinct block for each line of text, and I was able to create that, my CC file kept getting rejected. At first I thought it was the file type, so using 3Play Media's free file converter (bit.ly/2G6YpW4), I rendered the file in several different file types and resubmitted. Each one was rejected.

The real problem with this trial and error method is one of time. The converter renders the file instantly, and uploading the CC file takes just a minute or so depending on your internet speed, but it can take a couple of hours or days to find out that it has been rejected. As a result, it took me about a week to work out what was going wrong.

In the end, I figured out that the .srt file I was using was the correct one, but rather than being represented in neat blocks, it has to come out as one single very long line. Video Studio renders it in blocks, but "converting" it to a .srt file using the same 3Play Media converter (bit.ly/2G6YpW4) gave me a file that AVD accepted. This is what I discovered using my software. Your results may we'll be different with other video editing or Closed Caption software.

Art Requirements

You will need to provide Key Art and Background image files for use in the various menus in the Amazon system. For episodic series, you need three still images for each season plus an additional image for each episode. They can be variations of one another or completely different, but the aspect ratios are specific for each one required. This should be the easiest part of the entire uploading process provided you have images to use, but the one to accompany the individual episodes needs to be a 4:3 ratio. That one threw me for a minute or two since my software has a 3:4 but not a 4:3 preset. To solve this, I simply rotated the image 90 degrees, applied the 3:4 crop, and then rotated it back.

It should go without saying, but I will anyway: these image files should be as crisp and clean as you can make them. They may be viewed as thumbnails in some situations, but need to look crisp even on a big screen. Potential viewers will also be influenced by these images as they decide whether to try out your content. Help convince them with sharp, compelling images.

From Amazon Support, Art Requirements:

Standalone and episodic titles

o **Key art** *The image used to represent your title in search results, and title detail pages. On many devices where Amazon Video is available, we display cover art for standalone content (movies, featurettes, etc.) in a 3:4 aspect ratio; we display cover art for serialized content (TV shows, web series, etc.) in a 4:3 aspect ratio. To ensure future flexibility, we also require title artwork in 16:9 aspect ratio for both standalone and serialized images. Please submit .jpg or .png file format images at the following dimensions:*

o **Standalone titles** *1200x1600 (3:4)*
o **Episodic titles** *1600x1200 (4:3)*
o **Both standalone and episodic titles** *1920 x 1080 (16:9)*

o **Background images** *These appear on device detail screens. These images convey the mood of your content. Please submit .jpg or .png file format images at 1920x1080 resolution.*

For additional details and examples of key art, see the Graphic Assets Guide. (amzn.to/avdgxguide)

The only other item to remember with these images is that Amazon will not allow images containing nudity, violence, weapons etc. The shows can contain these, but the still images cannot.

From Amazon Support, Art Requirements:

Key art policy

Please adhere to the following key art restrictions. Artwork will be rejected if this policy isn't met.

- **Weapons**

We avoid using violence in Amazon promotions. The appearance of guns and other weapons isn't acceptable. If an alternate image isn't available, please use discretion. Additionally, avoid key art in which a weapon is pointing at the viewer or other figures within the image.

- **Violence**

If availability of non-gruesome imagery is limited, please choose assets with as little gore as possible.

- **Sex & Drugs**

Avoid images that depict drug usage, alcohol, nudity, or are sexually explicit.

Amazon Content Review

So, you finally got your video and Closed Caption files uploaded and have not been rejected on TECHNICAL grounds. You are not out of the woods yet! Your video still needs to be reviewed for content. In my experience, this takes 2 to 4 business days.

If your video is rejected for content issues, (or if it gets approved, for that matter) there is no direct notification. Once your complete package is submitted, the appropriate section of the "Your Videos" tab will show dots representing each Amazon region that your show is to be available in. These dots will show up half filled in green while it is accepted technically but awaiting content review.

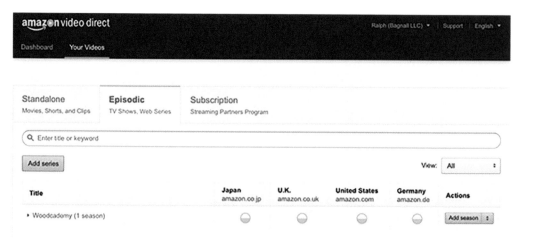

You will need to check in regularly to determine whether or not your show's status has changed. If you see the dots filled completely in green, *congratulations*, your show is streaming! My first episode went live sometime around 12:00 a.m. Eastern time, and I only know this because I was up late and checked before going to sleep. Honestly, after all the work and struggle to get the first episode online, I was so excited that it was quite some time before I finally did get to sleep!

For the initial upload of a program, the show will not be available for streaming until approval is gained. Once the show is approved, you can make changes to the show synopsis, key art images, or video and closed caption files. The green dots on your dashboard will turn half green again as the updates are reviewed, but your previously accepted files will continue to stream until the new approval is gained. Although this allows for ongoing updating of your content, go easy on this sort of thing. You do not want loyal viewers to be disappointed or confused by changes over time. (Han Solo really did shoot first!)

But if you discover errors in your video or Closed Caption file, fixing them and uploading a corrected file is desirable. Relevant additional information, company changes, etc., are important as well. For example, we created a new logo for Woodcademy, so I went back and uploaded new key art for both the series and individual episodes to ensure better images and more consistent branding.

If your content gets rejected, a marking in red will now appear on the dots. With your initial upload, the entire dot will turn red if it is rejected. If you have content already streaming and are adding a new episode, a red exclamation point will appear over the half-green dots. In either case, at the top of the page there will be a notice explaining the basic reason for rejection, and if you're lucky, a hint about how to fix it. Specifically, it will quote the relevant section of Amazon's support documentation. What it actually refers to may not always be clear to you, so you have to think like Amazon.

For example, my first submission was rejected a few times for "advertising". My show is about woodworking. I take the viewers through a project start to finish. While video is an awesome medium for this, it does not give the viewer crucial information such as specific dimensions. So I created a PDF set of plans that viewers can download free of charge from my website.

What took me a few tries to figure out was that even though I was trying to guide users to something free that would enhance their viewing experience, telling them to visit "www.Woodcademy.com" is advertising as far as Amazon is concerned. The Amazon Support Documents state that advertising "can" include a URL. I interpreted this as meaning that while a URL *might* be considered advertising, it might not *always* be so. What I ultimately discovered was that **a URL will always be considered advertising** and no URL may be used within the video, period. As soon as you say,"double-u, double-u, double-u, dot…", you can count on being rejected.

Through time-consuming trial and error, I ultimately found that telling viewers the plans can be found "on the homepage" got accepted. I am fortunate that the homepage is Woodcademy, the same made up word as the show title, so it is an easy find even without actually giving the URL. I also place the video clip mentioning the plans at the very end of the video, just before the closing credits. These credits *can* contain a written URL. So far, the written URLs I have included have not been rejected, so having one appear immediately after mention of the plans seems to work well for guiding viewers to the website. My plans have been downloaded repeatedly, so that's another usable metric.

You'll want to carefully plan out how to help folks find your domain if that is important to your business model. A future attempt to make direction to my website more obvious will be to display my web address in a sign on the rear wall of the studio area in my shop and see if it is rejected. If you need to experiment with what you can get away with, be scientific. Insert only one questionable item at a time, or else you may not know exactly why your program has been rejected.

Alternate Content

If the show you want to produce for AVD is a drama, comedy or other typical TV/movie fare, having alternative content available for your viewers may not be applicable. For shows that are enhanced by the availability of alternative content (woodworking plans with measured drawings in my case), then planning is necessary to help your viewers find and access your content.

In my case, having plans available for download and subsequent printing is rather important. Featured projects may require drawings, CAD files or similar content be made available to the viewer. Unfortunately, there is currently no method built into the AVD platform for managing this, and the restriction on advertising, including the mention of URLs, complicates the issue.

While I freely admit that part of the issue was my own fault, (once I read them appropriately, Amazon's support documents *are* clear about URLs) it seemed logical to me that the producer's own URL should be acceptable, especially as I was clearly guiding my viewers to free content that would enhance their viewing experience. After the first rejection, I sent an email asking why. Amazon sent a reply quoting *the no advertising policy* from the support files, and even specified the specific time of the infraction within the video which was rather helpful.

Perhaps I was being dense, but I sent another email explaining the value of the plans to the viewers and asking what they might recommend as a work around. The response repeated the "no advertising" information and then stated, *"Please be advised that we won't be offering any further insight or taking any additional action on this matter."* Lesson learned, be sure not to mention any URL or partial URL in the body of the show. So far, URLs in the closing credits have not been cause for rejection and, as I mentioned earlier, in a future experiment I plan to show the URL clearly on a banner in the background to see if that will comply with Amazon's restrictions on advertising.

It should be noted here that officially, URLs are not the only issue. The exact quote is "*…we do not accept any URLs, external links or calls to take action outside of the Amazon Video application.*" Certainly, there is a fine line to be drawn here, and only additional trial and error will allow me to more clearly define the specific boundaries. If your show, like mine, benefits from off-Amazon content, you will want to keep this in mind as you are shooting. The original URL mention that got my content rejected was part of a larger video clip that could not easily be cut to correct the problem, so I had to reshoot some footage. Anything I think might be flagged is now shot in its own clip and the same clip is shot without the experimental content, that way, if it is rejected, the clip can quickly be swapped out can easily be replaced without disturbing the natural flow of the episode.

As I mentioned previously, I was fortunate enough (believe me I did not know nearly enough to have planned this) to have the show title be the same as my website, and most folks can pretty easily make the connection. The name Woodcademy is a unique blend word, so it is easy for viewers to find my website even if they don't stick around for the credits.

Hopefully, you have the opportunity to think these things through a bit more than I did. If you will want your viewers to visit a website, you need to be strategic about the URL you want them to visit, and how you intend to let them know about additional content or why they might want to find your site.

These advertising restrictions make monetizing your video a bit tricky using AVD. Don't get me wrong, In general, I agree with their policy. The monetization difficulties will go a long way toward keeping AVD more exclusive than YouTube, but you will need to be thoughtful about how you go about making income from your show if that is your goal.

Monetization

mazon allows you to charge a fee to viewers who watch your video, which pays *"50% of net revenue"* by Amazon for each paid view. But in today's market, where loads of great content that viewers already know and love are free to watch, odds are slim that your program will be one they feel compelled to purchase. Even charging $0.99 is a HUGE psychological barrier for most people when compared to a FREE program choice.

From Amazon Support, Royalty Information, Buy or Rent:

Content providers receive 50% of net revenue. If you offer a season for purchase, customers who have purchased one or more episodes may be able to purchase the season for a discounted price. The season price is reduced by the amount the customer has already spent on previous episodes. You will receive 50% of net revenue for the episode and season purchases.

Under the free-to-view model you are paid on a per hour streamed basis at rates that vary based on minutes viewed. For content streaming free with a Prime account, a hit show may make enough to pay for itself, but for a niche show like mine, with many hours invested to produce each episode, that is a slow return on investment, if any return is ever realized using this model.

From Amazon Support, Royalty Information, Free with Prime:
Royalties for Prime Subscription Access will be paid according to the below rate card on a per title basis (for standalone titles and seasons) based on aggregate hours streamed by customers worldwide. Hours will start accruing when the title is streamed for the first time and will continue for a 365-day period. After the 365-day cycle, the streamed hours resets to zero and earnings will begin again at the lowest tier. We log and calculate customer streaming to the second.

Tier	Hours Streamed	Per Hour Revenue Rates (U.S.)	Per Hour Revenue Rates (UK)	Per Hour Revenue Rates (DE)	Per Hour Revenue Rates (JP)
1	0–99,999	$0.06	£0.04	€0.05	¥6.80
2	100,000–499,999	$0.10	£0.07	€0.08	¥11.30
3	500,000–999,999	$0.15	£0.11	€0.12	¥16.90
4	1,000,000+	$0.06	£0.04	€0.05	¥6.80

For all titles published before March 1, 2018, all hours streamed between September 1, 2017, and February 28, 2018, will be aggregated and used to determine a title's starting tier on March 1 (up to 500,000 hours). For example, a title that was streamed for 200,000 hours between September 1, 2017, and February 28, 2018, will start in Tier 2, at 200,000 hours, and earn $0.10 for hours streamed beginning March 1. This will be automatically applied to the rate that appears in the earnings report.

If you have chosen the *Free with Pre-Roll Ads* option for availability when you set up your account, you are paid 55% of whatever ad revenue Amazon generates from the advertisements they insert within your video. This is ONLY for viewers who DO NOT have an Amazon Prime membership, so they are unlikely to find your show through Amazon. **You need to figure out how to get the word to these viewers**. One way we do this is to clearly promote free viewing for audience members without a Prime membership on the website pages for the show, in any advertising we do or opportunities we have to promote the program in person.

Currently I am honestly not concerned about monetary return. My show is currently an experiment to determine whether or not demand exists for this type of program. My original plan was to prove the streaming numbers then approach sponsors to help pay for the show. But, as with most things, realities overtake the plans, in my case to my good fortune. Because I am one of the early adopters of AVD, and because I already have marketing relationships with several of the big names in the woodworking industry, there has been a surprising amount of interest in my show among potential sponsors. I've been actively talking about my show with them, and sharing the initial results which have been positive, so they are aware of what I am up to. Because we already have working relationships, it is much easier to bring up monetary sponsorship. In fact, a few are already discussing sponsoring Woodcademy after the release of just five episodes.

Since I cannot advertise within the show, and as far as I know I have the only dedicated woodworking show made just for Amazon Prime, setting a value to any sponsorship is tricky. I've been thinking hard about how I can promote sponsors and their products within the AVD guidelines.

Product Placement

Woodworking tool brands are typically distinctly colored and labeled, so most woodworkers watching the show will be able to easily identify brands I am using without me even mentioning names. And using the brand name casually and appropriately within the narrative has proven not to be a problem, but again, care needs to be taken.

I have learned not to ignore the background as I shoot. I created a studio corner in my shop where most of my filming is done. I built a modular wall system where I can hang tools so that the background is appropriate and pleasing to the eye without being cluttered. And the modular system allows me to quickly and easily change the items on view behind me in the frame, so I can do some product placement without actually using the tools.

Viewers on my YouTube channel have emailed me with questions about tools that briefly appear in a shot that had nothing to do with the tool they asked about. The background definitely gets noticed.

Apparel

Displaying branding on the clothing I wear is another value I can offer sponsors. I have a number of branded shirts from manufacturers that I wear when shooting product videos for them. I now make a point of wearing branded shirts when filming my show so that potential sponsors will see how visible branded wearables are. A few companies have sent me branded shirts to wear even though we have no monetary relationship, so this is a promising avenue for sponsorship. Once I bring sponsors on board, I will wear only their brands when filming, switching shirts so the brand matches the tools that are being used in a segment as much as possible.

If your show is a drama or sitcom, you may be able to get product placement fees for items like the cute handbag, scarf or blouse your leading lady wears, or the scotch your leading man prefers. Lesser-known brands are excellent prospects for approaching with these sorts of product placements.

One great example is that when Mars declined the opportunity to have M&Ms be the candy E.T. preferred, Reese's Pieces jumped at the chance and became a household name nearly overnight. This minor product placement made a huge impact on that brand and product.

I believe I can also place some unobtrusive signage on the backdrop behind where I shoot most of my video. Although I have not tried this yet, I have seen branded materials placed in the background of other independent AVD shows, so it appears to pass the AVD review process. Keep in mind that Amazon's primary objective seems to be that you not directly guide viewers to take action outside of the Amazon platform, but, so far, they seem less concerned about indirect marketing strategies.

Alternate Content

Now that viewers know to navigate to my website for additional content, I can offer exposure on the website, product plans and bonus content to sponsors.

I always have the ability to include sponsor branding, product information, and website URLs in the downloadable plans that accompany my projects as I have complete control over any companion content. Digital PDF plans can easily include links to products and tools shown within the videos.

The pages on my website, where visitors can learn more about my show and download the projects, are also mine to do with as I please. Beyond branding, I can offer sponsors the opportunity to place videos of particular products featured on the show, or other similar content of value to the sponsors within Woodcademy web pages.

Since beginning this process, I have also found that my YouTube channel can be used as a sponsor benefit as well. Almost every episode has footage I want to use but ends up being trimmed for time or clarity reasons. This can be repurposed as YouTube content marketed as Bonus Content on the Woodcademy website.

Some of this YouTube content is used strictly for marketing the show, but I also look for ways to promote my sponsors. For example, in Episode 3, I used some unusual clamps. I had originally filmed a clip explaining the clamps, how they worked for what I was doing at the time, and, of course, the manufacturer's name. I kept the part showing the clamps in use for the show production, but the deeper explanation hit the "cutting room floor."

This cut footage then became a YouTube video (bit.ly/2IDVm6o). I filmed a short opening shot saying, "In Episode three of my Woodcademy show on Amazon Prime, I used these clamps…", mentioning the show, the clamps and the manufacturer. On YouTube I can include URLs in my voice over, and links in the description; as my YouTube channel is now monetized, I get paid for those views through AdSense.

To find value for your sponsors, you will have to think a bit outside the box. For example, dramas on AVD could offer an online page with information about products featured in the episode much like a Marketplace section in a home or fashion magazine, and even include affiliate links so you can monetize any click-throughs.

Monetization will not be quite as simple as an AdSense account connected to your YouTube videos, but with some creative thought you can do quite a lot and benefit from less competition for the viewer's attention on AVD than you do on YouTube.

Sponsorship

I was originally planning to give the show about six months to see how the streaming numbers looked before contacting companies about sponsoring the show. As it turned out, within three months I had three major names interested in sponsorship. This is one of the advantages to being the first on a new platform, and it's a huge help that the platform is Amazon Prime. But again, money is not the focus of our efforts here at the beginning of my show, exposure is.

The trick is pricing the sponsorship program. Since this is an entirely new medium, and as far as I know I am the only person doing a dedicated AVD-only woodworking program, we are proceeding with caution. You always need to make you sure your sponsors realize greater benefit from their relationship with you than you charge them for sponsorship. This is tricky because sometimes it is VERY difficult to prove direct sales. If someone sees me using product X on my show and a month later buys it at their local woodworking store, how exactly do you prove the connection? More often than not, you can't, at least not through the show itself. Even if I could give out the sponsor's URL in the show (and we know that I cannot), there is no link for them to click that will record the connection. Not on Prime at any rate.

We are most likely going to offer packages to our sponsors that don't include payments to us for the first six months of our sponsorship program. We plan to provide them with exposure to our audience, and all the benefits we are able, including using as many trackable links as possible. In return, we will ask them to use their community, network, and connections to help market the show. At the end of six months, we will have some very definite numbers to help us decide what sponsorships are worth on a monetary basis. To do this, we are asking sponsors to provide links that they can track, and we use these whenever possible. If you don't have a trackable link from your sponsor, you can create one by adding UTM codes to the URL (Google Analytics has a Campaign URL Builder (bit.ly/2G8LbZ9) that makes this easy) or use a link service like bitly (bitly.com) to track links and show sponsors the traffic from your show or site to their website.

As mentioned earlier, this is where having online content to accompany your show can be extremely valuable. My website has a page for each season of the show with subpages for each project. There is an additional page for *Bonus Content*, the YouTube videos that augment the show. I provide free downloadable content such as project plans that viewers can use to follow along with the show. The website and the content are mine to do with as I please. Since they are not contained within the AVD system, I can add links to sponsor websites on my pages as well as the PDF plans. These links can be completely trackable to give sponsors metrics they can use to determine return on investment well beyond the placement of their products on my show.

Additional content on YouTube is also valuable as YouTube numbers are very easy to show potential sponsors. You can easily prove that, say, 1000 viewers are watching your video connected to the Amazon show that mentions a particular product. You can include a trackable link in the description and prove actual engagement. The more you can show how viewers are directed to and clicking through to the sponsor's website, the more valuable sponsorship is.

Getting Found on Amazon Prime

You've figured out all the technical and content issues and your program is now streaming. *Congratulations!* All you need now is for people to find it.

In more than a decade of producing video content for myself and my clients, I believe firmly that **content is king**. No amount of publicity will save your show in the long run if it stinks. On the other hand, compelling content will keep viewers coming back even if your production values aren't Hollywood quality. But for all that, you still need to get eyes on your show.

At this time, there is no provision in Amazon Prime for adding keywords, tags or other search terms to your programming. My show is a woodworking show, but doesn't appear in a search on Amazon for "woodworking". I enquired by email about this issue and the reply was, *"The "woodworking" keyword is only in the synopsis, so the title is not searchable by "woodworking". You should be able to find the title by title name."*

This means that, for the time being, the show titles themselves are the only searchable terms within AVD. If I had titled my show "Woodworking with Ralph", the search would be easier for my potential viewers using "Woodworking" as a search term. But as I explained in the section on content review, that name would have made finding my website, and the plans to go with the show, that much harder.

Again, giving some though to both your show titles and domains can get you the best of all worlds, great search results within Amazon and great conversion rates to your website if that is your purpose.

I was invited to complete a survey sent to me following up on my interaction with Amazon Support, and I certainly took that opportunity to point out that adding some method of applying relevant search terms to the show listings would be of benefit to the viewers as much as to producers. But for now, understand that titles are all that matter for search on Amazon Prime.

So, how to go about getting eyes on the show?

The usual suspects, Facebook, Twitter, Pinterest, Instagram, etc. are a great place to start. I will not bother with giving instructions for all the usual Social Media channels. There are thousands of books on the subject, and I am less expert than their authors. But depending on your subject matter, there are lots of creative ways to get word out about your show.

Facebook is, of course, the 800 pound gorilla in the room. Your show simply must have its own page, and you should participate on as many group pages as possible, just be sure that they are relevant to your subject matter. Post regularly on your page, keeping in mind relevance to your show and audience. If you can afford it, promote your posts to reach potential new viewers too. Facebook promotions are fairly inexpensive, so this might be a great way to get your info out there. There are many other social media platforms you can use as well, but you should concentrate on those that will best engage the key audiences for your show. For example, if your show has applications for business, **LinkedIn** might be a venue to utilize.

Be sure to connect with **online groups or boards** that align with your subject matter. My show is about woodworking, and the members of the online woodworking groups that I have long participated in became the original core audience of my show. Those early viewers were key as they contributed to the seven 5-Star reviews we received within our first 60 days. This initial kick-off proved to be VERY useful when I began talking to sponsors about the show.

While we increasingly live in a digital world, do not neglect the power of **print outlets** as well. Hobby or trade magazines that are similar to your subject matter still get a lot of eyes, and psychologically, being mentioned in a printed magazine still carries weight. A press release sent to the right people can reap real rewards for getting your fledgling show noticed. Woodshop News is a major trade magazine for the wood industry, and a short mention in their weekly e-Zine brought a measurable bump in viewers to the show and visitors to my website. A well thought out press campaign can bring in viewers.

Of course, having an existing community of followers to reach out to is a big help. I have an active **website** and **YouTube** channel and I already write freelance woodworking articles for hobby and trade magazines. All of this was helpful in attracting viewers to the show early on.

If your show is of local interest, you could write short articles based around your show's subject matter for local newspapers. Most major metropolitan areas also have at least one glossy magazine devoted to the area. The editors of these magazines are always looking for fresh content. If you can help them out with an interesting article or two that are not just sales pitches for your show, they will be responsive. This is a great way to get your name out and confer some "expert" status on yourself. It's surprisingly effective if done right.

Amazon Prime helps to promote your show as well. They provide show producers with an AVD Marketing Kit that includes a variety of Amazon branded icons and logos for use in promoting your programming. Additionally, much like they do in their retail model, Amazon offers the audience suggestions based on what others have viewed. At the bottom of my show's Prime listing is a section titled "Customers who watched this item also watched", where a variety of other woodworking-related shows (some nationally known) are featured. If you go to the listing for one of those shows, it is likely that my show is being cross-promoted to their audiences by Amazon, all at no cost to me.

Paid Advertising

One of the next steps for me is buying advertising in a few woodworking magazines. Done right, this can be effective and not too expensive. How well print advertising may work for your show is something to consider. Remember, you need to promote your show where your target audience is. For you, print might be a good fit, but your best bet might be any of a number of other advertising methods like Pay Per Click, targeted email promotions, online banner ads, direct mail, trade show appearances, and social media campaigns to name a few.

Sponsor Networks

I hope to work with my sponsors to market the show to their audiences. Fortunately, I already have a working relationship with several well known companies in the woodworking industry, so there is a lot of opportunity here. Normally, I'd need to prove the viewer numbers before inviting sponsors to pay for exposure to my show's audience. But because I already have a working relationship with the companies I would like as sponsors of my show, there has been significant interest on their part even before the numbers prove out. One told me that "wherever this journey leads, we want to be part of it," which is pretty exciting, especially at this early stage.

Final Thoughts

Amazon Video Direct is a very unique resource at the moment. At some point, other television and streaming services may launch similar services, but for now AVD is the only game in town for independent producers to get their movies and shows out to the television-viewing public. I was excited to find it and start using it for my show. I have no idea where this will go in the long run, but the ride is proving to be great fun so far. I'm also very interested to see the things creative folks around the world will do with the service as its availability and popularity continue to grow. I can see it becoming a fabulous resource for product training, education, entertainment, and utilized in ways no one has yet explored.

As you work to develop your own show on AVD, I invite you to reach out and let me know about your programming as it makes its way onto Amazon Video Direct.

About the Author

Ralph Bagnall is a woodworking professional, author and the host of Woodcademy TV, available exclusively on Amazon Prime. In his 30 years in the industry, Ralph has worked closely with a number of woodworking manufacturers and retailers to produce written and video content to support and promote their products and brands.

He and his wife, Susan, live in Southwest Florida.

Discover more about Ralph Bagnall at Woodcademy.com and ConsultingWoodworker.com.

Printed in Great Britain
by Amazon